Contents (Third Edition)

The Ramblers promote country walking, protect rights of way, campaign for improved public access to the countryside, woodlands etc. and defend the beauty of the landscape. The Ramblers play a major role in securing legislation to protect our paths and countryside. Please give your support by becoming a member. Write to:

The Ramblers
Camelford House, 87−90 Albert Embankment, London SE1 7TW.
Tel 020 7339 8500.   **Fax** 020 7339 8501.
email ramblers@ramblers.org.uk   **website** www.ramblers.org.uk

Berkshire Area
There are a number of Ramblers' groups across the county, each of which arranges its own programme of walks and other events. For details of the individual groups go to www.ramblers.org.uk/berkshire.

Cookhamdean Common and Bisham Woods

A few well-farmed fields, lots of wild woods, a couple of inviting pubs; mainly on the high ground overlooking the Thames Valley above historic Bisham. An opportunity to enjoy some of the many square miles of woodland across the country, where public access and sensitive management is ensured by the Woodland Trust.

Distance: 6¼ miles / 10 km
OS Map: Explorer 172 Chiltern Hills East
Start: Winter Hill viewpoint car park (Grid ref: SU 870 860, Postcode: SL6 9TN)
The walk may also be started at Cookham Station (increasing its length by ¼ mile) but parking time is limited to 1 hour. (Grid ref: SU 887 851, Postcode: SL6 9BP)

Having savoured the view (and perhaps an ice cream!) with your back to the car park turn right along the road past Dial Place, before turning left down a byway – Job's Lane. Cross lane into sunken footpath and after another crossing lane go straight up the common ahead, shortly bearing left up a chalky track leading to, and then beside, the Green at Cookham Dean.

1 At War Memorial turn right along Church Road and then left on track beside church and burial ground. Follow churchyard wall to waymarked drive (a public path), passing Huntsmans Cottage. After swing-gate join fenced path, known as Kennel Lane, towards distant roofs of Cookham. At bottom of track go ahead into High Road and, immediately after passing school, turn right into Alfred Major Recreation Ground. Keep fence of school on right and where this ends bear half-right to exit at gap about halfway along top boundary of field.

If you wish to return to the station, do not turn into the Recreation ground but continue along High Road to the station. To reach this point from the station, see map.

2 Cross garage area and follow estate roads round left and right bends until, just before T-junction ahead, turn left beside green strip, then carefully cross road ahead into Lesters Road. Shortly turn left and find (unsigned) tarmac pathway between Lesters Cottages. Swing-gate leads to path between fences which shortly crosses wide gravel track and goes straight ahead between fields, to emerge at road (Long Lane).

3 Turn right up road, using verge

Marlow and the Thames from Quarry Woods

where possible. At top of field on left (pausing to admire view towards Windsor Castle) at parking area turn left on grass path beside hedge. Bear right into next field, still with hedge on right until, when level with metal gates, turn half left across field. At corner of wood ahead (Beeching Grove Wood) continue to corner of field, through gate and on between trees. Facing open field ahead, turn right, with wooded strip on right. About halfway along second side of this field turn sharp right on woodland path. Reaching corner of property ahead go through swing-gate (ignoring the permitted path) and bear right on winding path to end of woodland, opposite house known as Butlers Gate.

4 Keep to verge on right into Choke Lane before crossing to NT sign and onto wide track. At open common, bear left on path along left side of common, passing solitary tree, with road nearby on left until, a few yards before parking area, turn left through gap in hedge to cross road onto wide track. Follow this past buildings of Park Farm. Shortly after large property at beginning of woods ahead,

turn right through gap beside wooden gate and a notice 'Bisham Woods. Woodland Trust. Welcome'. This is Inkydown Wood, the beginning for us of a 1½ mile sweep through Bisham Woods.

5 Follow the main path, later sloping down, soon with fine views over Thames-side Bisham village and towards Chiltern Hills. Keep to main path as it descends, increasingly steeply, finally down to major path junction in deep gulley. Here turn half-right up stony bridleway, shortly keeping left at first fork. Before top of gulley, fork left onto footpath, to climb more steeply. After some distance, the footpath bears left (at white waymark arrow) and continues along edge of ridge, dropping steeply to road. With great care walk up road for 50 yards, then cross over and take narrow path, close to road at first. Stay on this mainly level path to emerge on drive to "Rivendell" and, just ahead through bushes, the viewpoint on Winter Hill, our starting point.

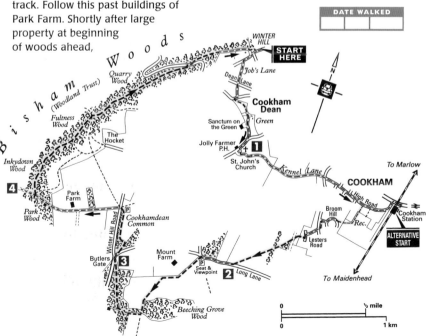

Maidenhead Thicket and Pinkney's Green

Enjoy the freedom to roam over the 850 acres of commons and greens, once part of the Saxon Royal Manor of Cookham, now in the safe keeping of the National Trust. Highwaymen are rare today in the Thicket but there is wildlife a-plenty in its leafy glades. Part of the waymarked Maidenhead Boundary Walk is included in this ramble.

Distance: 5½ miles / 9 km
OS Map: Explorer 172 Chiltern Hills East
Start: National Trust parking area off Cannon Lane, Maidenhead. (Grid ref: SU 859 803, Postcode: SL6 4QQ) See map for alternative start at Furze Platt School.

Facing footpath sign, take left-hand path (of three) along the broad grass ride ahead, with boundary hedge of Maidenhead Thicket on left. Where main ride swings right, keep straight on along narrow path passing buildings on left (Claires Court School). Cross tarmac drive and descend steps (cut in 1975 by scouts of Maidenhead Boyne Hill troop) and along path through old chalkpit to swing-gate and turn right along road (Cherry Garden Lane). The first of several Maidenhead boundary stones on this walk is just ahead, outside Heathside Cottage, corner property on left.

1 Go ahead along lane and just before main road (A4) bear right, cutting across grass strip to use traffic-island over road, then follow footpath ahead into Maidenhead Thicket. At prominent crossing ride, continue ahead then as path bears right, bear left on path into trees. Soon cross avenue of mature trees and carry on to end of Thicket woodland. Just ahead descend slope and go under road bridge before bearing right up slope and along a ridged path to road. Another stone is on nearside verge to left here.

2 Cross road into broad grass ride ahead. *You may like to add a short detour (few minutes each way) to view the attractively situated Stubbings Church, by taking the gated path on left just before first house ahead.* Try to spot the next boundary stone tucked away just right of wooden gate of Leigh Cottage. Now continue along roadway (Darling's Lane) to a junction. On the island here used to be a damaged Boundary Stone; can you find it?

3 Continue ahead for some 85 yards and look for another stone on left, just beyond entrance of Greenlands. Pass last house, St Timothee's, and shortly ahead follow edge of Pinkney's Green, then gravel drive. At road ahead turn left for about 60 yards, then left again, to find another stone, by start of footpath, plus two 'boundary nails' embedded in nearby oak tree. Return to road, cross to Golden Ball Lane and fork left along gravel track past Fairwinds. After wooden rails fork right beside wooded NT common. Reaching cottage on right go straight ahead across green and road to enter Malders Lane.

Follow lane, noticing NT Brick & Tile Works on right. At buildings of Hindhay Farm turn right, across concrete yard in front of farmhouse, to go through swing-gate ahead, fenced at first, then widening to mid-field path. On far side of field, after swing-gate, turn right behind buildings (Littlewick Farm) and follow drive. Where boarded fence on right stops, turn right beside it and after a few yards aim half-left across field, to cross the road by '40' and speed camera signs.

4 Stay near road along edge of common at first, then bear right, beside line of bushes on left. Pass to right of large chestnut tree and nearby cricket green. Shortly after end of trees on left, follow path straight across common, aiming just right of white(ish) house (beside tall chestnut tree) and speed de-restriction sign. Cross Bix Lane into a gravel lane and follow footpath signs back onto common, keeping road (Moorlands Drive) nearby on left. Reaching road junction, cross Pinkney's Drive, to follow left-hand edge of common, finally to reach roundabout on Bath Road. Cross ahead onto footway. Where this shortly joins roadside, bear left along wooded strip. Meeting road (Sandisplatt Road), turn right to rejoin footway beside Cannon Lane, following it under road bridge, before crossing with care to return to start.

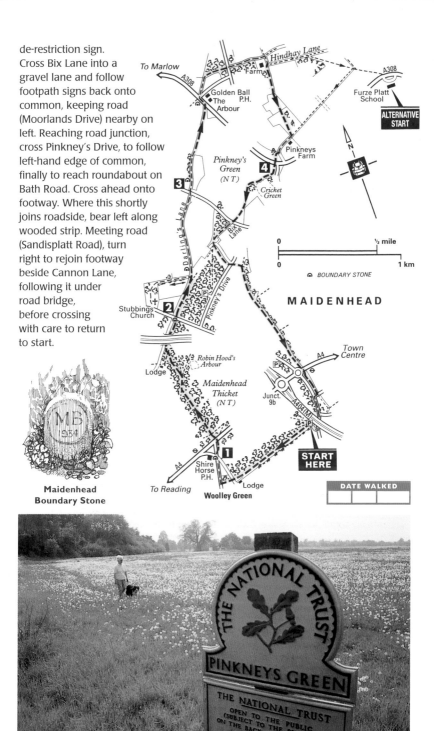

To Marlow

Hindhay Lane

A308

Farm

Furze Platt School

ALTERNATIVE START

Golden Ball P.H.
The Arbour

Pinkneys Farm

3

Pinkney's Green (N T)

4

Cricket Green

N

Darling's Lane

Bix Lane

0   ½ mile

0   1 km

⊙ BOUNDARY STONE

MAIDENHEAD

Pinkney's Drive

Stubbings Church

2

Robin Hood's Arbour

Lodge

Maidenhead Thicket (N T)

Town Centre

A4

P

Junct. 9b

A404(M)

START HERE

A4

1

Shire Horse P.H.

Lodge

To Reading

Woolley Green

DATE WALKED

MB 1954

Maidenhead Boundary Stone

This green was acquired by public subscription in 1934

Woolley Green and Shottesbrooke

Whilst a sea of 20th-century development now laps up close to one of Berkshire's most historic houses, the 15th-century Ockwells Manor, it still provides a peaceful start and finish to this walk. But the high spot for many will be the medieval church at Shottesbrooke in its splendid parkland setting.

Distance: 8¼ miles / 13 km

OS Map: Explorer 160 Windsor, Weybridge & Bracknell

Start: Ockwells Park Car Park, Cox Green, Maidenhead (Grid ref: SU 878 790, Postcode: SL6 3YU)

Turn left out of car park and walk towards Ockwells Manor, then on to end of this quiet lane. Here cross over, turning right, then left at mini-roundabout into Highfield Lane. *If you want to know how long it takes to walk exactly one kilometre, check your watch now, then look again when you reach the end of this road at Cannon Lane.*

1 Cross Cannon Lane and by side of Thatched Cottage pub enter Firs Lane which soon narrows, becoming a field-path with hedge on left. At end of field go straight on, soon through woodland path. At end of field go straight on through woodland path. At end of path, go through swing-gate then carry on in half-left direction across small field to leave by wooden gate. Join concrete track to reach road, in the hamlet of Woolley Green, one of several Greens once in Windsor Forest.

Turn left along lane until, opposite large colour-washed house, turn right up slope. Cycle path ahead soon crosses road (to Business Park) and continues as wide farm track with views over hedge on right to Ashley Hill (474 ft.) and on left to distant spire of our objective, Shottesbrooke Church. Where path turns left, ignore first path through field, ignore second path on left at three-way fingerpost and carry on to next diagonal field-path on left with road/railway bridge in distance. *Overhead the sound of light aircraft from White Waltham flying club often competes with the skylarks!*

2 On far side of field, climb up gravel path to reach road on railway bridge. Turn left, passing Shottesbrooke Farm. Follow winding road, which eventually straightens, with flint-built lodge on right. Turn right here through metal gates along tree-lined drive and, where trees end, the path line bears left on grass, to join tarmac drive passing in front of house to reach the splendid Church of St John, inspired by Salisbury Cathedral and unaltered since its completion in 1337.

3 From church kissing-gate, follow

Ockwells Manor

line of path from stone waymarker, across park left of pond (sometimes dry). After stile on far side, path narrows through wooded strip and by side of field, to reach cricket field. Unless visiting The Beehive pub ahead, turn right, round edge of field, pass behind pavilion and cross road into Walgrove Gardens. Keep left of green, then pass right of house ahead and go through metal gate. Turn left, keep left of first field, go through metal gate, then along right side of field above, to turn right along lane in front of Waltham Place.

Follow lane (Church Hill) passing fountain commemorating 60 years of Queen Victoria's reign. At junction (B3024) go ahead for 100 yards and turn left through swing-gate to follow left side of two fields. Entering third field turn left, still beside wood. In field corner turn right, and look for large wooden gate on left, at entrance to wooded path. Emerging in field ahead, turn left for 15 yards, then go through swing-gate and along right-hand field edge, soon joining wide track (Snowball Hill).

Church of St John, Shottesbrooke

4 Turn right at junction and pass buildings of Heywood Farm. By first house on right, turn right along field-edge until, at start of trees, turn right along wooden walk-way under power lines. In field ahead, turning right, follow ditch at first, heading towards Ockwells Manor in the distance. Eventually, at end of field, go through pair of gates and bear left along unmade Thrift Lane. At end, turn right and follow road to return to car park.

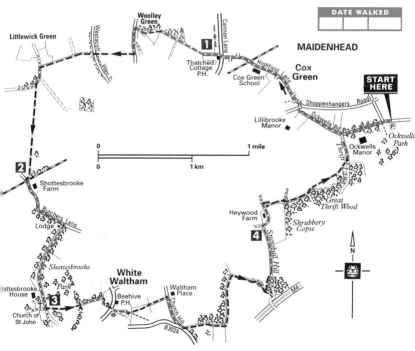

Littlewick Green and Prospect Hill

Sample two of East Berkshire's unspoilt villages and climb the quiet woodland path to enjoy the panoramic view from Prospect Hill, overlooking the Thames at Hurley to the Buckinghamshire Chilterns.

Distance: 5 miles / 8 km
OS Map: Explorer 172 Chiltern Hills East
Start: By Village Hall, north side of Littlewick Green
(Grid ref: SU 838 812, Postcode: SL6 3QX)

Facing the Village Hall with its sundial inscribed:

'Tis mine the passing hours to tell
'Tis thine to use them ill or well!

turn left and then right into Coronation Road. Continue for some 60 yards, then opposite Larbet Cottages turn left into narrow fenced path. Path goes straight ahead along field-edge, then beside track, before passing farm buildings of Frogmore Farm. Continue across open field to kissing-gate in hedge on far side. The path line here continues straight ahead across pub garden. Pass to right of tall car park hedge and over strip of common to cross Bath Road at traffic island. Go down steps and soon turn right along middle of wooded common, keeping field close by on left.

1 Cross a drive and bear right on woodland path. Where this almost reaches lay-by for a bus-stop, turn left across short boardwalk and join a wide path ahead with thick woodland (Ashley Hill Wood) on either side. We shall be following this footpath, in the same direction, for about 1 ½ miles. You will soon reach a gravel drive, turn left. The footpath continues a few yards ahead on the right. Shortly re-cross gravel drive to continue on footpath immediately ahead. Soon, beside wire–fenced reservoir, our path forks half right, dips into a hollow, and comes to a track. Turn left. The footpath continues 25 yards ahead on the right, before finally descending though trees to emerge at lane opposite Ladyplace Cottages.

Ashley Hill Wood is part of the Forestry Commission's Chiltern Forest and was leased in 1951. Its 80 hectares (200 acres) was largely re-planted during the fifties with a variety of species, including oak, beech, pine and spruce.

2 Go through metal swing-gate to left of cottages and follow right side of meadow. Ignore ladder stile by metal farm gate and at bottom corner of field pass through two metal swing-gates and then on across next field to

Hall Place *Painting by John Manson*

wooden gate. Cross bridleway then concrete farm track and head towards distant trees (High Wood). Go straight through this wood leading to the splendid viewpoint on far side, known as Prospect Hill.

Now turn right along edge of woodland (Bisham Church in view half-left). Path bears right back into the wood (*follow footpath not permitted path*) before emerging to dip down across the farmland, heading straight towards the buildings of Hall Place and Farm. *This is now the home of Berkshire College of Agriculture. Please ensure you follow the path and do not stray onto the college campus.* Path becomes a track and keeps right of farm buildings before narrowing between fences, to join tree-lined concreted avenue.

3 Reaching front of Hall Place mansion (built 1728-35) turn left onto main drive for a short distance, before forking right through gate where signed footpath runs diagonally across field. After a metal swing-gate continue on grass path, then a metalled drive, leading past a cluster of cottages and old houses to reach the centre of Burchett's Green, opposite the Crown. Cross over, bear right along the road, and continue to Burchett's Green Infant School on your left.

4 Turn left immediately before parking area beside school and onto woodland path which will shortly bear left over common emerging at Furze Cottage. At roadside turn right. *Across the road here you will see the unusual dove tower of Stubbings Manor.* Look for bridleway forking right off lane, opposite Old Oak Farm.

Appropriately called Green Lane with view of Ashley Hill on right, it leads to the Bath Road (A4). Just before main road, cut across corner of common on left, so as to cross road via traffic-island. Go ahead into Jubilee Road and at beginning of green turn right into Gilchrist Way to return to the start.

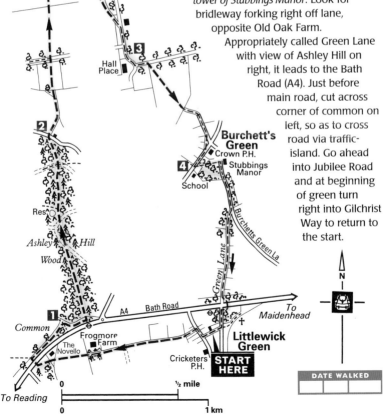

PROSPECT HILL
High Wood
Hall Place
3
2
Res.
Ashley Hill
Wood
1
Common
Frogmore Farm
The Novello
Cricketers P.H.
Burchett's Green
Crown P.H.
4
Stubbings Manor
School
Green Lane
Burchetts Green La
A4 Bath Road
To Maidenhead
Littlewick Green
START HERE
To Reading
0   ½ mile
0   1 km
N

DATE WALKED

Ashley Hill and Dew Drop Inn

This refreshing walk begins by climbing to the summit of Ashley Hill (474 ft) with fine views back over Berkshire. Visit Brakspear's tucked away Dew Drop Inn, once a simple ale-house, now with a fresh lease of life for the 21st century.

Distance: 3¼ miles / 5 km

OS Maps: Explorer 159 Reading, Wokingham and Pangbourne and 172 Chiltern Hills East

Start: Lay-by on north side of Bath Road (A4) at Knowl Hill (Grid ref: SU 822 794, Postcode: RG10 9UR)

Facing the A4 turn left along footway, passing Village Hall. At lay-by beyond last building bear left over parking area to road ahead (Warren Row Road). Cross road, pass metal barrier and bear left over strip of common to metal kissing-gate. Here in Bottle Meadow aim up through middle to exit at field-gate in far top corner.

From here go ahead up drive for 35 yards, then through kissing-gate on left into field corner.

1 Follow wire fence on right, shortly to cross stile ahead and go uphill with hedgerow on right. Go through farm gate into next field and continue climbing, now with hedge on left. Go through kissing-gate at top corner and enter woodland path, narrow at first, soon becoming wide track, winding up to the top of Ashley Hill. *This is the site of a one-time Victorian keeper's cottage, now sadly over-developed since being auctioned by the Forestry Commission in 1987.*

From top of hill continue past house to path junction and turn left quite steeply downhill with views through trees to far horizon. A few yards beyond wooden barrier turn right, along level bridleway. Pass old gate and some 50 yards ahead turn left down to Dew Drop Inn.

2 From pub continue down bridleway, pass through a gap in the fence then immediately turn left over

Loddon Valley Ramblers near Pudding Hill

footbridge, then left again along fenced path round a plantation to highest point of field. Pass through a kissing gate. The path now continues round edge of field, but you may prefer to take direct line to far side (permitted path). At this point turn left up track for 50 yards, then take second footpath

Bluebells in Lot Wood

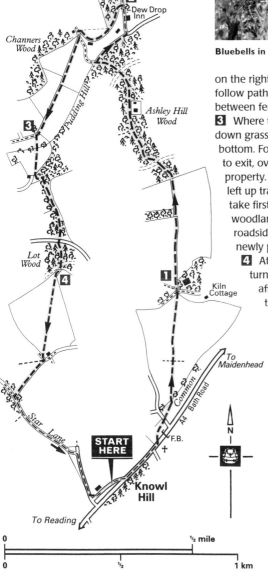

on the right through wooden gate to follow path ahead, becoming a track between fences across paddocks.

3 Where track bears right, turn left down grassy slope to cross stile in field bottom. Follow path between fencing to exit, over a stile, just left of property. In front of this house turn left up track for a short distance and take first footpath on right through woodland strip, leading down to roadside. Cross ahead into area of newly planted trees, Lot Wood.

4 At end of newly planted trees, turn right on to gravel path and after 40 paces turn left through swing-gate. Entering next field ahead, go diagonally across it, aiming left of distant trees, to exit at swing-gate in corner. Turn left for 20 paces, go through swing-gate on right and follow hedge. Leave field at swing-gate and a few yards ahead turn left into top end of Star Lane, to follow ribbon of homesteads downhill towards the mounting rumble of traffic along Bath Road.

Channers Wood

Pudding Hill

Ashley Hill Wood

Dew Drop Inn

Lot Wood

Kiln Cottage

To Maidenhead

Common

A4 Bath Road

Star Lane

START HERE

F.B.

Knowl Hill

To Reading

N

0		½ mile
0	½	1 km

Bowsey Hill and Juddmonte Farm

Hills, woods, meadows, fields and a climb to the top of tree-clad Bowsey Hill, a landmark visible for many miles around. Stroll beside peaceful paddocks of an internationally famous stud farm.

Distance: 4½ miles / 7 km

OS Maps: Explorer 159 Reading, Wokingham and Pangbourne and 172 Chiltern Hills East

Start: Lay-by on north side of Bath Road (A4) at Knowl Hill. (Grid ref: SU 822 794, Postcode: RG10 9UR)

Facing the A4 turn right, cross Star Lane, and (biting the bullet and braving the traffic noise) hurry along the short distance beside the A4 before turning right into the quiet haven of Canhurst Lane! Follow rising right of way through an old iron kissing gate, along a woodland strip to reach a wooden swing-gate.

1 The path straight on has been officially diverted for some years to come to enable mineral working to take place. So turn left along the stony track provided as an alternative, soon dipping down. At bottom of gulley the diverted path climbs to right but instead continue ahead beside wide plank bridge (nearly hidden) and follow a permitted path meandering through woodland, to emerge at gate and junction with bridleway. Here turn right uphill, soon joining raised path beside Lindenhill Wood, a route believed to have Roman origins. At top of climb continue ahead, now on a level restricted byway to Crazies Hill, leading past scattered properties on upper slopes of Bowsey Hill.

2 Path joins descending roadway (Hatchgate Lane), soon with view on right of substantial house, Cayton Park. At crossroad (known as Holly Cross) by lodge, turn right along quiet lane. At next crossroad go straight on into Rose Lane, looking for kissing-gate shortly on right. Take this path, soon beside paddock. *The thoroughbred foals often seen grazing here in the early months of each year may be racing on the famous courses of the world three years later. Pick the winners now!*

3 The path turns sharp left along next side of this first paddock, then right, across wide grass strip, passing the immaculate brick and flint buildings of Juddmonte Farm, (formerly Pudders Farm). At end of buildings turn left along tarmac drive until, where this turns left, go straight ahead across grass to gap in corner. Path descends beside hedge to pair of gaps at bottom of slope where we have a choice of ways.

4 For the 'summer route', perhaps, go through further gap in fence ahead and turn right along tree-shaded old bridleway, known as Hodgedale Lane. *This was once used by local tradesmen driving their traps between Warren Row and the Henley Road.* In winter, you may prefer

Our route beyond Lot Wood

the drier option by turning right along the parallel grass path, to the end of the paddocks, then turning left through kissing-gate to join Hodgedale Lane.

Either way, the old lane soon joins a broad farm track, becoming a concrete roadway past cottages. Keep left of grass triangle (signed Pudding Hill) and go straight on along road (facing traffic) and where this swings left, go straight ahead into trees of Lot Wood.

5 Cross footbridge and go through metal kissing-gate, then turn left along side of meadow to leave via another kissing-gate in far top corner. Hedged track leads to isolated cottage. Go round wooden farm gate on left and in front of the cottage turn right through third kissing gate and aim for right-hand end of trees ahead. From this point field-path descends diagonally to final kissing-gate by houses. Join track ahead which soon leads back to start.

Spindle-tree alongside our route

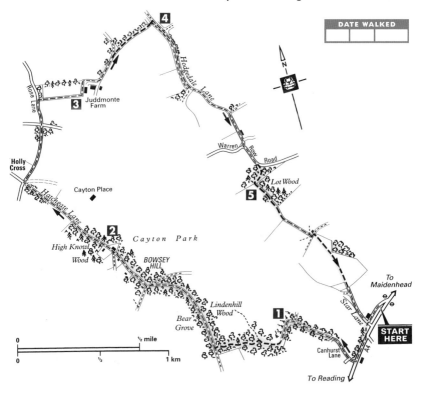

High Knowl Wood and Penny's Lane

The hamlet of Crazies Hill has changed little in the last hundred years. The sometimes hilly paths we use today through the small fields and quiet woods still provide the views familiar to the Victorians in 1900 who hauled the materials from nearby Henley-on-Thames to rebuild the former Georgian Town Hall (of 1795) in its new country setting. This walk can be muddy, so do go suitably prepared.

Distance: 4 miles / 6 km
OS Map: Explorer 171 Chiltern Hills West
Start: North end of Crazies Hill Road by C of E. Primary School. (Grid ref: SU 799 808, Postcode: RG10 8LY)

With your back to the school turn right along footway. Just past entrance to Crazies Hall (the former Town Hall, see above) cross road and turn left beside village hall, keeping left into narrow path, hedged at first. At end of grass path beside paddocks, cross through gate and turn right along quiet lane.

This soon slopes down and at bottom of dip turn left through gap beside metal gate and go ahead along path beside wood, soon bearing slightly right between two large trees. Waymarked path (painted arrows) climbs steadily ahead with fir plantation (part of High Knowl Wood) nearby on right.

1 Eventually, path descends to junction. Here go straight on over two crossing tracks as path dips down. Path winds ahead, passes through two defined fence gaps. Improved path surface steadily ascends until, with swing-gate 25 yards ahead and sawmill in sight, turn right, downhill. At one point, notice down through avenue of trees on left a large house known as Yeldhall Manor.

2 Towards bottom of slope, path crosses stream before re-crossing to reach swing-gate ahead. Now bear right, down side of rough field, before turning right on signed path into wood, crossing narrow ditch and ahead to footbridge, soon followed by wooden stepped boardwalk. Path ascends slightly, with fir trees in wood on right, then levels out. At

Penny's Lane

path junction go through gap ahead to descend down mid-field path, across line of oaks, to stile onto road.

Turn right along lane as far as end of field (by Highfield Farmhouse), and turn left over stile in corner. Within a few yards bear right onto gravel track. Where this track turns right between wooden posts, follow wide curving grass track ahead which climbs over a low hill. After crossing a stile follow avenue of mature trees leading down to another stile by gate. Keep near ditch and copse on right to leave field in corner and continue along edge of garden of bungalow (Penny Green) to emerge at road.

3 Turn right along road for some 30 paces then turn sharp left down restricted byway (Penny's Lane). Follow this old sunken track for about ½ mile, bending sharp left at about the half-way point.

4 At end of long field on left (part of golf course), by wooden field-gate, turn right up bank to squeeze-stile and climb uphill alongside fence on right. At top of hill pause to enjoy fine view towards Henley in the river valley and the Chiltern Hills beyond. Keep along top of pasture (with handsome white house in view ahead) before dropping down to leave field by rusty swing-gate. Now bear right, up narrow lane, past house named Worleys Hill and, shortly, pass Worleys Farm.

5 Follow lane and turn right over stile by first tree in group ahead. Take path through two fields, towards left side of prominent white building (that old Town Hall again!). Path ahead goes alongside private orchard to leave corner of second field via kissing-gate, leading to road, close to our starting point.

DATE WALKED		

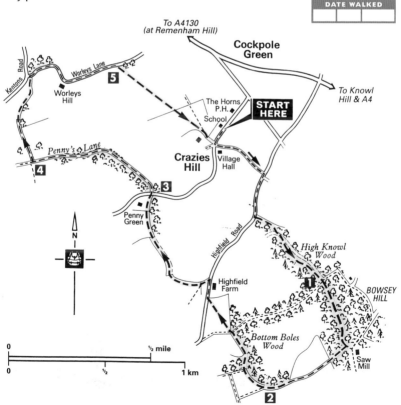

Rebecca's Well and Bottom Boles Wood

An easy climb through fields and tracks to the modest heights of Crazies Hill, a hamlet which seems to have side-stepped the 21st century. From the charmingly decorated well, saunter along old paths through older woods, finally along a new field-path back into thriving Wargrave.

Distance: 5 miles / 8 km
OS Map: Explorer 171 Chiltern Hills West
Start: Recreation Ground, off Victoria Road. Wargrave. (Grid ref: SU 794 786, Postcode: RG10 8BG)

From recreation ground walk back down Recreation Road and turn left down Victoria Road. Notice on left the posh entrance gates of 'Woodclyffe Allotments 1903', before crossing over to turn right up Purfield Drive and following it to the top. Here turn right (Blakes Road) for 50 yards and cross over to metal kissing-gate and follow footpath half right. At corner of field, cross footbridge and turn left along field-edge, with hedge on left.

1 At lane ahead (Highfield Road) turn left for 100 yards, then join headland path in field on right and after some 200 yards turn left at FP sign, taking mid-field path to road. Turn right along road (Crazies Hill Road) and then 40 yards past drive entrance of Hennerton Golf Club turn left through kissing-gate. Stay close to hedge on left and in far corner descend via steps, then continue across golf course to kissing-gate. At bottom of valley turn right onto rising bridleway (Penny's Lane). *How many centuries did it take to carve out this ancient, sunken track joining Crazies Hill to the Henley Road?*

2 Finally reaching road, immediately turn left between field-gates onto footpath through wooded strip, with scattered cottages of Crazies Hill in view across field to right. Soon look out on left for a possible glimpse of Crazies Hall in its spacious grounds, with recently formed lake. *This elegant Georgian building served as Henley-on-Thames's Town Hall, overlooking the market place for nearly a century before being taken down in 1897 and re-erected here. It obviously enjoys its retirement!*

Emerging opposite Village Hall, turn right along road and where this dips

Rebecca's Well

down, bending right, go straight on into a gravel byway past Rebecca's (delightful) Cottage. Before entering footpath shortly on right, go ahead for 25 yards to view Rebecca's Well. *This spring used to be the hamlet's water supply. In 1870 the curate of Wargrave, Rev. Greville Phillimore invited subscriptions to build this pictorial well-head.*

Returning to footpath, follow it through copse and up to kissing-gate at field-side. Head straight across to railed stile in far corner. When narrow path on roadside bank descends, continue along lane until, just beyond the yard of Highfield Farm, go through kissing-gate on left and continue up middle of field past line of oaks. At path junction at top of field go straight on, beside firs on left, before descending a stepped board-walk to footbridge over gulley (Bottom Boles Wood).

3 At grass field ahead turn right along one side before turning left into hedged bridleway known as Green Lane. Follow this track as far as end of field on right where a swing-gate marks a permitted path (see our map for alternative route) which shadows the copse then descends over open grassland to kissing-gate. *See notice about path status under Countryside Access scheme – still valid in 2016.*

4 Descend Hanover Gardens and turn right along footway leading around the estate of Highfield Park to reach Blakes Road. Turn left for some 30 yards and cross road opposite two metal gates. Go through gates, but if locked, turn right into Kings Acre. Immediately turn right again, through a swing-gate onto a fenced path. Turn left and continue to wooden gate on the right and enter the playing field. Cross to the far left corner of the field, to the left of the BMX course, to reach gates into recreation ground and the well-tended greensward at start.

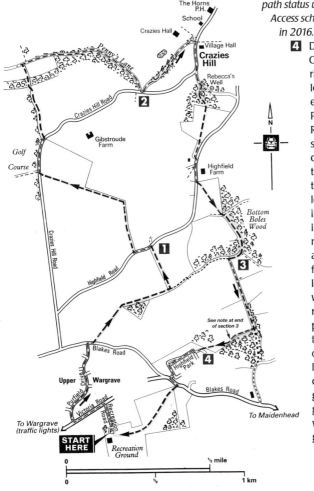

The Horns P.H.
School
Crazies Hall
Penny's Lane
Village Hall
Crazies Hill
Rebecca's Well
Crazies Hill Road
2
Gibstroude Farm
Golf Course
Highfield Farm
Crazies Hill Road
Bottom Boles Wood
1
Highfield Road
3
See note at end of section 3
Blakes Road
Highfield Park
4
Upper Wargrave
Purfield
Victoria Road
Recreation Road
Blakes Road
To Maidenhead
To Wargrave (traffic lights)
START HERE
Recreation Ground

N

0   ½ mile
0   ½   1 km

DATE WALKED

Ruscombe Church and Mumbery Hill

If you have an hour or so to spare – morning, noon or summer's evening – this short walk on good paths across open farmland can be followed in either direction, with return by train taking just 4 minutes (Usually an hourly service.)

Distance: 3 miles / 5km

OS Map: Explorer 159 Reading Wokingham and Pangbourne

Starts: Twyford Station
(Grid ref: SU 790 758, Postcode: RG10 9NA)
Wargrave Station
(Grid ref: SU 781 784, Postcode: RG10 8EU)

Twyford Station to Wargrave

Leave station forecourt by path beside ticket office. Carefully cross road, turning right across bridge and at start of hedge turn left into playing-field (Stanlake Meadow). This Permitted Path follows the railway then swings right to gate. Here turn left along tree-shaded lane, over railway, then bear right on slip-road just before crossroads. Keep turning right (into Church Lane) and walk between the trees towards St James the Great, Ruscombe.

In front of church bear left along lane and at crossroads go carefully over into Castle End Road. Within 100 yards fork left on bridleway up metalled drive, and shortly turn right immediately in front of gates at Northbury Farm. *The group of listed buildings here includes the (just visible) timber-framed Elizabethan manor house of Northbury, sympathetically restored in 1988/89.* At end of field on right, follow bridleway over New and London Roads, heading diagonally across open field to far right corner. In next field follow line of trees on grass strip, then ahead on gravel to the Bath Road (A4).

Carefully cross road, go through bridle-gate, and follow track (passing soft fruit and poly tunnels). Reaching road (Mumbery Hill) turn left along footway until, just before first property on left, turn left (by seat) onto descending field-edge path. At first corner of field keep right, beside garden fences, with burial ground in one-time chalk pit below on right. At fork in footpath, where houses appear on left, take right hand path and on reaching unmade road, cross to tree-lined path on right of Orchard End. At main road (A321) turn right, then shortly left, into Station Road, at the end of which is the station.

May Day celebrations at Ruscombe Church

From Wargrave Station to Twyford

Join footway bearing right onto Station Road passing, at one point on left, the elegant war memorial by Edwin Lutyens on the Green (access here also to the church, village landing stage and three pubs). At end of Station Road turn right and cross over. Shortly ahead turn left, in front of Leafy Lane House, into tree-lined rising path. Reaching unmade road either go straight ahead to view burial ground in old chalk pit or go a few paces right to go up, between concrete posts, into narrow path beside garden fences on right. At corner of field continue ahead leading up field-edge to road (Mumbery Hill). Here bear right along footway until, just before first house ahead on left, turn right into wide track, passing poly tunnels, leading down to Bath Road (A4).

Cross with great care, pass left of gate and straight on over gravel to follow line of trees ahead between fields. At corner of next field route follows diagonal line to far side. Here bridleway crosses London and New Roads and continues beside field now with hedge on right. This is an old way, as well as our way, to Ruscombe Church. *On the left along here, notice path into small wood, 5 acres of one-time osier beds now cared for by FORWOOD – Friends of Ruscombe Wood.* Pass over stone stile by gate, and turn left down Northbury Farm Drive.

Reaching lane, facing pair of cottages, bear right and shortly cross into Church Lane. Either follow church fence bearing right or cut through the pretty churchyard. Follow lane, noticing Ruscombe Lodge (the vicarage in Victorian times), bearing left on slip road before crossroads. *Double hedge along here hides 'Penn's Garden', recalling William Penn, founder of Pennsylvania, who spent his last few years at nearby Ruscombe House (now demolished).*

Cross railway bridge and within 100 yards turn right and cross playing-field to exit in right-hand corner. Turn right over railway bridge, then immediately left down tarmac path to station.

To Henley
R. Thames
St. Mary's Church
Greyhound P.H.
WARGRAVE
Wargrave Station
Cemetery
N
Seat & Viewpoint
Mumbery Lane
Sheeplands Farm
A4
London Road
Local Nature Reserve
Northbury Farm
Ruscombe
TWYFORD
START HERE
B3024
St James Church
To Maidenhead
Twyford Station
To Reading
Rec.

0   ½ mile
0   1 km

Pitlands Farm and Weycock High-road

Share the view from Knowl Hill enjoyed by the Romans who once lived in this area. Follow the old tracks leading to Waltham St Lawrence, a Saxon village owned in 1006 by Ethelred the Unready. This is an easy, level walk but can be very muddy after wet periods so, unlike the King, do go suitably prepared!

Distance:	4½ miles / 7 km
OS Map:	Explorer 159 Reading, Wokingham and Pangbourne
Start:	Lay-by on north side of Bath Road (A4) at Knowl Hill. (Grid ref: SU 822 794, Postcode: RG10 9UR)

Facing the A4, turn left along footway, passing Village Hall and use footbridge to cross A4. From school entrance walk forward 30 paces and turn left through wooden gate to cross corner of churchyard. Turn left up lane for 50 yards then bear half-right across grass strip to join well-used path up through trees to emerge at top of Common, with bench seat nearby and extensive views to Windsor Castle, Ascot racecourse and even on a clear day to the tower at Canary Wharf.

From seat take the clear path down hillside towards far left corner of Common. Cross road, go a few yards along drive, then turn right along edge of Common with hedge on left. Turn left along lane past house and buildings of Lower Lovetts Farm. At junction of three ways, take the stony, middle (footpath) route. Go straight on past sub-station, becoming field-edge path, with hedge on right at first, later on left. At road (Bottle Lane) turn right. Where road turns left (notice this unusual cottage) go straight ahead into gravel drive of Pitlands Farm.

1 After house, path continues ahead on grass path. Pass between wooden posts and continue along field-edge beside hedge. Stay on field-edge until it swings right. Here go straight on, over railway footbridge. Continue straight ahead on field-edge for some 200 yards, where a finger-post indicates path leaves headland, turning some 30 degrees right across large field to swing-gate in far corner, just left of large house (former Victorian vicarage). After this gate turn left, then shortly right into Halls Lane, leading down to village centre, perhaps taking path across corner of

... leave headland to follow line indicated across large field

churchyard to admire the incredible 17th century 'Wilkinson's Yew'. *The 14th century Bell Inn was given to the church in 1608 by Ralph Newbery, Lord of the Manor, who was Master Printer to Queen Elizabeth I.*

2 To continue the walk, turn right immediately beyond lych-gate and cross stile beside gate to Wheatsheaves. The well-signposted right of way shortly bears right, passing in front of farmhouse, then threads its way between farm buildings to emerge on a broad track between open fields, with the twin peaks of East Berkshire ahead, Bowsey to left, Ashley to right. Re-cross railway at bridge ahead.

In 1847 the field on left, known as Weycock Hill, was excavated to reveal the remains of an octagonal Roman temple, similar to one at Silchester. The temple here may have been an important religious centre for the many villas known to have existed in this area. At one time the way from London left the main road at the 29th milestone and ran across here to the village, being known as Weycock High-road.

3 Where track divides by solitary tree bear right, leading to swing-gate to left of trees (Effie's Copse, named after the late Miss Effie Barker, an indefatigable local fox-hunter). Continue ahead on bridleway, conveniently shielded by hedges on both sides from wayward golf balls. Eventually track reaches a road. Turn right for a few paces, then

climb steps up bank, go right on drive and into narrow path between garages, leading to edge of Knowl Hill Common. Take a few paces left, then turn right and go straight across the common to trees on far side, beyond which hides white-painted Hope Cottage. Turn left along lane, past Royal Oak just ahead, leading back to A4 and the start.

The Green Lanes of St Lawrence

Little has happened to alter the farms and fields round this old Saxon village since the vicar, Thomas Wilkinson, planted his yew tree in the churchyard in 1655 and in the same year Mabel Modwyn was 'arraigned for witchcraft and condemned'. Unusually, the church owns the village pub!

Distance: 5½ miles / 9 km
OS Map: Explorer 159 Reading, Wokingham and Pangbourne
Start: Waltham St Lawrence Parish Church, in centre of village. (Grid ref: SU 829 769, Postcode: RG10 0JJ)

With your back to church lych-gate (facing ancient pound) go forward to Neville Hall and turn right along Milley Road. Taking due care of the traffic, pass houses at first, then open field on left. At end of this field bear left onto bridleway beside The Old Press. Follow track (Nut Lane) finally to emerge and turn right, crossing over, along wide verge (Twyford Road). Follow iron fencing to end of field on left and,

opposite St Lawrence Orchard, turn left through metal swing-gate onto drive. Follow path-line through a series of these gates, at first along hard track beside fields, then on grass field-path, ending at swing-gate beside wooden shelter, next to a hedged track (Mire Lane).

1 Here turn right along surfaced track, passing West End Farm and, shortly, Viners. At road junction turn left, soon passing colour-washed former Plough Inn. Beside Fornells (on right-hand side of road) bear right along Bailey's Lane for short distance, then at second drive turn right onto path beside timber-framed Bailey's Cottage. This hedged track leads to path junction facing open field. Go ahead over footbridge into field and straight on for some 150 yards to another two bridges. Now continue through copse (bluebells in May!) with deep ditch on left, leading to road.

2 At road (Hungerford Lane) turn left for 60 yards, then go through wooden gate on left and head across middle of field to gap in hedge on far side.

On the woodland path leading to Hungerford Lane

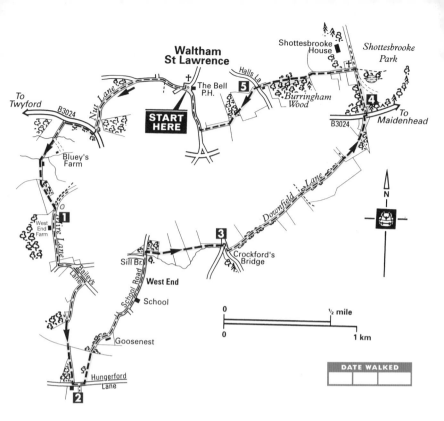

Woodland path passes left of 'Goosenest' cottage and continues along gravel drive. At road turn right and just ahead, at junction with Brook Lane, go straight on along footway of School Road, through the hamlet of West End.

Just beyond side road on left cross Sill Bridge and immediately turn right through swing-gate to join footpath, beside panelled fence at first, then straight on through a series of swing-gates over three meadows, then behind handful of houses to reach road by Crockford's Bridge.

3 Cross ahead over both roads then turn right for 30 yards to join bridleway, Downfield Lane, on right-hand side of property. Follow this old green lane for about ¾ mile until finally, where track turns sharp left, cross stile ahead and bear slightly left through field to exit at stile beside metal field-gate and on along grass

track. At roadside turn right, crossing over, to enter bridleway into Shottesbrooke Park.

4 Keep shallow ditch on left to reach drive ahead in front of medieval church of St John, beautifully kept and remarkably unaltered since it was built in 1337. Turn left through metal kissing-gate and follow flagstoned path past church porch and ahead between high brick walls. Path continues between field and ha-ha (a cunning device of fence in a man-made ditch to preserve an open view, in this case from Shottesbrooke House). At corner of wood ahead continue in next field along edge at first, then through trees to road (Halls Lane).

5 Cross straight over where path ahead follows series of wooden kissing-gates, finally passing beside allotment gardens to road. Here turn right along footway of The Street, back through village to start.

Stud Green and Blackbird Lane

This easy, level walk from the delightful old village of Holyport is through tranquil countryside ranging from lush meadows to trim polo grounds. It can be muddy after wet weather so do go suitably shod.

Distance: 4½ miles / 7 km
OS Map: Explorer 160 Windsor, Weybridge & Bracknell
Start: War Memorial on Holyport Green (Grid ref: SU 892 778, Postcode: SL6 2JL)

With your back to the War Memorial, turn half-right over middle of Green and cross road (A330) to enter footpath to left of hedge alongside white-painted house (formerly The Cricketers). After concrete footbridge, follow right-hand side of field ahead (beware of boggy areas). Go through two gates in hedge and take path forking left, keeping close to left-hand hedgerow through next three fields, passing small pond on your right. In fourth field, keep following hedge until it turns sharp left then continue in same line across field to gate on far side. Path ahead goes over wooden footbridge and then

through gate to follow left side of field. Approaching large house, keep to left of boarded fence to emerge on roadway at Stud Green.

1 Turn left and after several properties turn right into Rolls Lane. Where track ends at metal farm gate ahead, turn left through wooden barrier into narrow footpath, soon with hedgerow and ditch on left. After gate into field, continue ahead beside hedgerow. Some way along field (currently a polo ground), just beyond gateway on left where track joins, turn left through gap in hedge, and take diagonal line through three fields to metal kissing-gate at road (A330) in far corner. Cross over busy road, turning right, towards Touchen End.

Soon, immediately after The Poplars cottages, turn left on concrete farm track, which soon swings left. Facing gateway to Foxley Court Farm, turn right along conifer-lined track with paddocks on right. Eventually, at end of conifers, turn right along track – Long Lane.

2 Continue to large white house on left, go 35 yards beyond it and turn left over footbridge onto grass path round two sides of house grounds, then turn right, becoming field-edge, with hedge

The Green at Holyport

on right. At end of this field turn right, and go straight ahead on wide grass track over open field. Shortly, path turns left with deep ditch on left at first and continues to end of big field. Cross over footbridge and continue beside fencing before turning left over white-railed bridge and along tree-lined bridleway – Blackbird Lane – where you may well hear one!

3 On reaching road (B3024), turn right for some 120 yards and directly after Old Beams Kennels, turn left into hedged track known as Primrose Lane. Follow this old way for nearly ½ mile until, about 200 yards beyond pond beside path, turn left and cross plank footbridge. Keep right of field, beside ditch at first, then follow track to road (Moneyrow Green). Cross over into Bartletts Lane which continues as tree-lined track. Reaching main road (A330) ahead, turn right on gravel path along edge of Holyport Green to return to start.

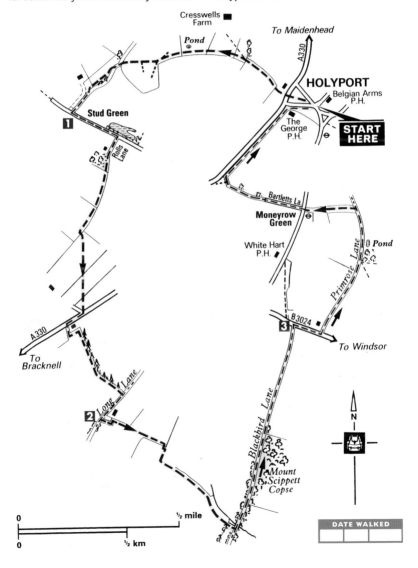

DATE WALKED

Fifield and Gays Lane

This wedge of surviving countryside in the historic parish of Bray is surprisingly thinly populated, giving a feeling of remoteness despite its nearness to Maidenhead and Windsor. The walk forms a double loop, linked together in Fifield village, offering an easy shorter alternative.

Distance: 3¾ or 5½ miles / 6 or 9 km

OS Map: Explorer 160 Windsor, Weybridge & Bracknell

Start: War Memorial on Holyport Green. (Grid ref: SU 892 778, Postcode: SL6 2JL)

Facing the War Memorial go ahead along Holyport Street past pond and Belgian Arms. At end of road go through gate and turn right through field to swing-gate at roadside. Carefully cross over and head along Stroud Farm Road until, after last bungalow on left, turn onto surfaced footpath, soon beside avenue of conifers. Coming to a corner area turn half right, then right again through swing-gate and over culvert.

The rising ground ahead has been reclaimed after mineral extraction,

enabling access to be re-opened on the original line of the right of way and now providing wide, open views from the higher ground.

1 From this point, keeping fenced hedgerow on right all the way, follow path almost straight ahead through several fields for about ¾ mile, and finally emerge at roadside, beside terrace of cottages. Here turn left along Coningsby Lane to T-junction just ahead.

For the shorter walk turn right here through Fifield village, past 'Hare & Hounds' (see map). Continue to path on the right, at section 3 below and follow sections 3 and 4 back to the starting point.

2 To continue the longer walk turn left at T-junction (Fifield Road) until, beside last property on right (a nursing home), turn into a footpath between hedgerows. At end of 'tree tunnel' section continue into field with hedge on right. Path later turns right between hedges then swings back left. Cross

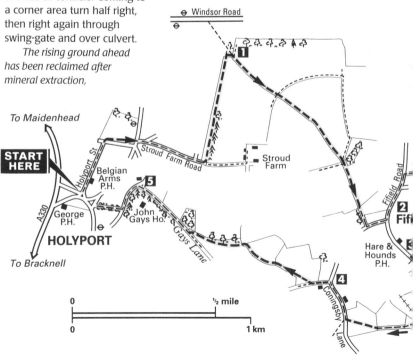

Coningsby Lane *Painting by John Manson*

first footbridge in corner and turn left into hedged strip. At path T-junction turn right for some 75 yards where path continues between hedges. At end of enclosed section turn right to cross open field and leave over culvert, to continue ahead along side of next field. Immediately after junction of paths turn right onto field edge path with hedge on left, and walk through several fields (often muddy) to emerge finally in village (where short walk re-joins – see map).

3 Cross over, turning left along footway until, just beyond pair of houses turn right into drive, signed Deep Meadows on gateposts. In front of pillared wooden gate shortly ahead turn left onto narrow wooded path. *The whole length of this path was impenetrable until 1971 when it was cleared by members of the then newly-formed East Berks group of the Ramblers.*

Emerging at metalled road, almost immediately turn right (opposite Ledger Cottage) to reach swing-gate into field. Path ahead leads beside paddocks until at road turn right (Coningsby Lane again) shortly passing house and barn.

4 Where road swings right, follow surfaced bridleway on left. After 100 yards turn right over stile beside metal farm gate. Turn left beside fence and hedgerow, cross stiles and footbridge into field corner. Continue beside left-hand hedge in next field. On left, cross pair of stiles and bridge over ditch into meadow, then pass cluster of oaks to stile in far corner. Turn right along metalled track, called Gays Lane.

5 Where track forks, keep left and turn left along road (Langworthy Lane) for about 150 yards. Immediately past gateway of John Gay's House, turn right into footpath (known locally as the 'Click Clack' and reputedly haunted!) which leads back to Holyport Green.

DATE WALKED

Hogoak Lane and Tickleback Row

Explore the wedge of unspoilt, quiet countryside still to be found between Maidenhead and Bracknell. Our circuit starts in Warfield, at St Michael's Church (one of Berkshire's finest) and strides on through fields and green lanes. The length of the walk can be reduced to 6½ miles by a short cut via Hawthorn Hill (see map).

Distance: 8¾ miles / 14 km
OS Map: Explorer 160 Windsor, Weybridge & Bracknell
Start: Parking area opposite Warfield Church. (Grid ref: SU 880 723, Postcode: RG42 6EE)

Facing Church turn left along Church Lane, cross to kissing-gate into first field on right, next to Vicarage. Go half-left over two paddocks to kissing-gate in hedge and continue in same line to footbridge in bottom corner. Here path has been diverted to follow line of stream on left, marked by metal 'rambler stileways'. Go up beside steps and turn left (over Wane Bridge) up lane, shortly turning right through metal swing-gate on fenced path into field. Follow this clear path straight ahead,

... continue ahead on field-edge

past farm buildings on left, until finally reaching road, by Brockhill Stables.

1 Turn left up footway, towards hamlet of Brockhill, before soon turning left along short concrete drive. Pass houses on right, then bear right over yard to broad grass track, beside ditch and hedge. Continue ahead, still beside hedge on right, passing through gate finally to reach road. Cross ahead into Garson's Lane. Follow this quiet country road and just beyond bend by Old Whitelock's turn left. *See map for shorter route, which continues straight on from here.* To continue the full circuit, shortly ahead turn right into Hogoak Lane.

2 Follow Hogoak Lane, a delightful old tree-lined byway which passes a BBOWT nature reserve, Chawridge Bank, for more than a mile before reaching Drift Road, a one-time drove-road to London from the west. Here turn left, crossing over, and take hedged path on right, just past two modern houses (replacing a cider house). Reaching open field ahead, turn left through middle of field to go through double gates. In next field cross ditch between white metal rails, join track ahead to find gate in hedge, just right of brick stable. Now cross bridleway and continue ahead on field-edge, dotted with splendid mature oaks marking the way, with a right-hand kink in second field. About 75 yards along headland of next field turn right at waymark post, and through gate, to head half-left across field towards stile on far side, just right of white-gabled house (Long Lane Farm).

3 At stile, immediately turn left along hedged bridleway. Reaching metalled road turn right, soon becoming grass track. After metal gate, keep along left side of field leading into hedged path to road. With great care cross over into Sheepcote Lane, to take footpath before first property on left, the drive to 'Windmills' where, immediately left of house, pass through gate in hedge and continue in same direction on grass path. After 'dog leg' to right carry on, soon passing through yard to road. Here cross over, turning right, and continue for 100 yards to cross footbridge over ditch and join a field-path at metal gate. *This path was opened as a Right of Way in 1998 following much research of old records by local Ramblers' stalwart, Robin Mosses.*

4 Path follows field-edges, with road on right at first, includes two right and left turns, but stays beside ditch until in final field ditch runs ahead into trees and path turns left, soon with more open views of The Cut, a much more appealing stream than the name suggests! Exit field by a kissing-gate just before a

ford, to join track straight on ahead. *Footbridge to right over stream leads to nearby Westley Mill.* Follow hedged byway (Hazelwood Lane), pass caravan park and then go straight on as byway continues. Look for first house on left, behind hedge, and turn left along roadway through hamlet of Tickleback Row, emerging at crossroad by Shepherds House.

5 Cross ahead into Bowyers Lane, past Moss End Farmhouse. Roadway shrinks to single track and we fork right, before turning left at Frost Folly Country Car Park. Keep left of the car park and follow metalled track through right and left turns. Near top of rise, by large tree, turn right through swing-gate, shortly to return to car park at start.

To Maidenhead

B3024

Bridge House P.H.

Sheepcote Lane

A330

Long Lane Farm

3

Braywoodside

DATE WALKED

Drift Road

4

Drift Road

The Bourne

The Cut

Ford

Pendry's Lane

HAWTHORN HILL

Hawthorn Lane

Ashmore Lane

Hopgrove Lane

Chawridge Bank (BBOWT Nature Reserve)

2

Hazelwood Lane

Old Whitelocks

Garson's Lane

Shepherds House P.H.

5

Tickleback Row

Buckle Lane

Moss End

START HERE

A330

To Ascot

0 — 1 mile

0 — 1 km

P Warfield

Church

The Cut

Wane Bridge

Brock Hill

B3022

1

To Bracknell Town Centre

N

Monks Alley and Orange Hill

Despite recent development, Binfield retains its own distinctive rural charm, seen best from the leafy 'green lanes' we follow, with so many interesting properties, new and old, large and small. The map shows two loops forming shorter alternative routes (not described in the text).

Distance: 4½ miles / 7km

O.S. Maps: Explorer 159 Reading, Wokingham and Pangbourne and 160 Windsor, Weybridge & Bracknell

Start: Small parking area at Wick's Green, accessed along gravel drive beside 65 Stevensons Drive, off Terrace Road North, Binfield. (Grid ref: SU 841 714, Postcode: RG42 5TD)

Take path in left corner of parking area, cross bridge over ditch and follow surfaced path (over Silver Jubilee Field) to turn left along quiet lane, called Wick's Green. Shortly turn right into Monks Alley. After Angel Farm on right the lane shrinks to a leafy bridleway, leading to a T-junction. Here turn right onto steadily ascending track (Green Lane). Reaching top look across road (Carter's Hill) offering 90 degree views towards Ashley and Bowsey Hills with Chiltern Hills in far distance.

1 Turn right up tree-lined road past Warfield Garage on your left. Carefully negotiate bend past Billingbear Lane and follow wide verge beside high wall of Billingbear House. *(Footpath leaving road beside East Lodge offers short-cut back to start.)* Further ahead along road, turn left at cottage along drive to Orange Hill House.

2 Where tarmac finishes and drive swings right, take footpath tucked in hedge on left. Cross two fields (there are often horses in the first field) with 'rambler stileways' each end (a feature of the countryside around Bracknell). After second stileway, keep to right of hedge ahead. Emerging on narrow lane, turn right, leading down to junction with busy B3018. Here turn left for a few paces then cross over into hedged bridleway.

3 At the top of this lane turn right past the buildings of Hill Farm and along a straight tarmac drive (a public

Angel Farm   *Painting by John Manson*

The Ramblers protect your right to walk in the countryside

You can help by becoming a member

Write to:
Camelford House, 87–90 Albert Embankment, London, SE1 7TW
Email: ramblers@ramblers.org.uk
Tel: 020 7339 8500

ramblers
at the heart of walking

bridleway) emerging beside Stubbs Hill football ground, opposite cemetery. Turn right up hill and shortly continue ahead on footway leading to Binfield's 14th century parish church of All Saints, on the hillside. *The gravelled drive to car park beside church offers a glimpse of the splendid former Rectory.*

To continue walk, we recommend crossing road from outside 'Birdsong Cottage' which used to be All Saints School. Continue along footpath turning left into Terrace Road North, soon passing 'Jack O'Newbury' *(a pub*

since 1730, named after a famous and wealthy cloth merchant in Henry VIII's time − 'a man of merry disposition and honest conversation!')

4 Footway ascends and near top of slope, cross carefully into Wick's Green. Just beyond two houses ('Wordley' and 'Chestnuts') set back from lane, bear right into field-edge strip and then turn left along second side of field to re-join road. Turn left for a few yards then right, through a swing-gate, to follow perimeter path to left, round Wick's Green open space, leading back to start.

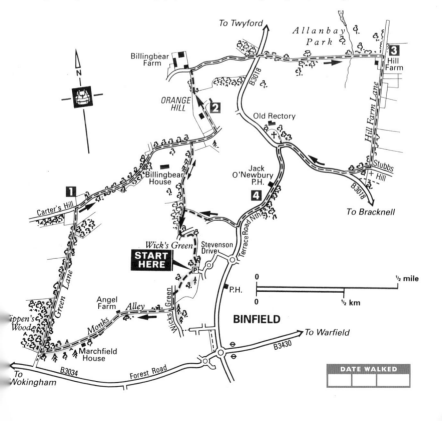

The Cut through Winkfield

An easy, level stroll through the lush green meadows still surrounding the historic centre of old Winkfield, with its medieval church and centuries-old coaching inn. Cross (twice) the diminutive Cut, a tiny stream reputedly home to the ubiquitous minnow and stickleback.

Distance: 3½ miles / 6 km

OS Map: Explorer 160 Windsor Weybridge & Bracknell

Start: Playing-field car park, junction of Forest Road/ Chavey Down Road, at Winkfield Row. (Grid ref: SU 897 711, Postcode: RG42 6LY)

Leaving car park, turn right and follow footway past restaurant and assortment of houses on right until, at end of wall to Grove Lodge, turn right into Grove Lane.

1 At far end of lane, by white cottage, turn right through swing-gate into path beside meadow. Keep to this continuously fenced path (there is little choice!), leading beside the fields and over a stream (the Cut). Note the so-called 'rambler stileway' here and others along the walk. At top of final field, faced with a choice of ways, turn left along an old route called Parker's Lane, with prefabs on right.

At wooden gate ahead, go straight on along narrow roadway, soon to turn right on gravelled footpath (just before Appletree Cottage). Shortly pass Millstone Cottage on left and go straight on along grass path, hedged both sides. Continue through a metal swing-gate then along fenced path to the road. Cross road in front of the 'Cinnamon Tree Restaurant', turning right along footway – Maiden's Green.

2 Where road soon forks, bear left along Winkfield Street, passing an assortment of village properties, including the Winning Post pub. Just beyond 'Old Timbers' turn right into narrow fenced path. Enter corner of field and within a few yards, by power-pole, join the path bisecting the meadow. After swing-gate into next field, follow the fenced path to reach stile beside metal gate. From this point head for church (12th century St Mary's, Winkfield) via a swing-gate to find a second swing-gate into churchyard. Follow wall to road and cross over, turning left in front of pub.

A stop at Winkfield to refresh body and soul

Along the churchyard wall note the arched brick gateway to Old Rectory House, built at same time as nearby church tower. The cost of the tower in 1639, replacing a wooden one, was £181 2s 10½d. If open, do view inside of church where the roofs are supported by five oaks dated 1592. See also Wild Life and Millennium windows. The White Hart Inn was originally the manorial court-house of Winkfield, becoming a coaching inn in the more recent past.

3 From the White Hart follow footway until, at end of wooden fence, beside tall iron gates, turn right into grass footpath, soon with hedges and fields both sides. Entering field ahead follow fenced path, hedgerow trees on left, and at bottom corner cross sleeper-bridge. Emerging at roadside (Braziers Lane) turn right, using verge wherever possible until, immediately past bridge (Coopers

Bridge over the Cut), turn right through swing-gate, joining fenced path as it goes round two sides of large field before turning right. Follow the fenced track, passing through three swing-gates, finally to reach wooden gate. Here note the unusual carved stone heads, high on the end wall of Hollington House. Now turn left, completing our circuit. Retrace your steps along Grove Lane, turning left along Chavey Down Road and so back to car park at start.

We can see gables
the lawn with tables
the barn and stables
of the old White Hart,
the car wheels crunching
the people lunching
drinking, and munching
their apple tart.

An extract from 'The view from the tower' by Simon Baynes, former Vicar of Winkfield.

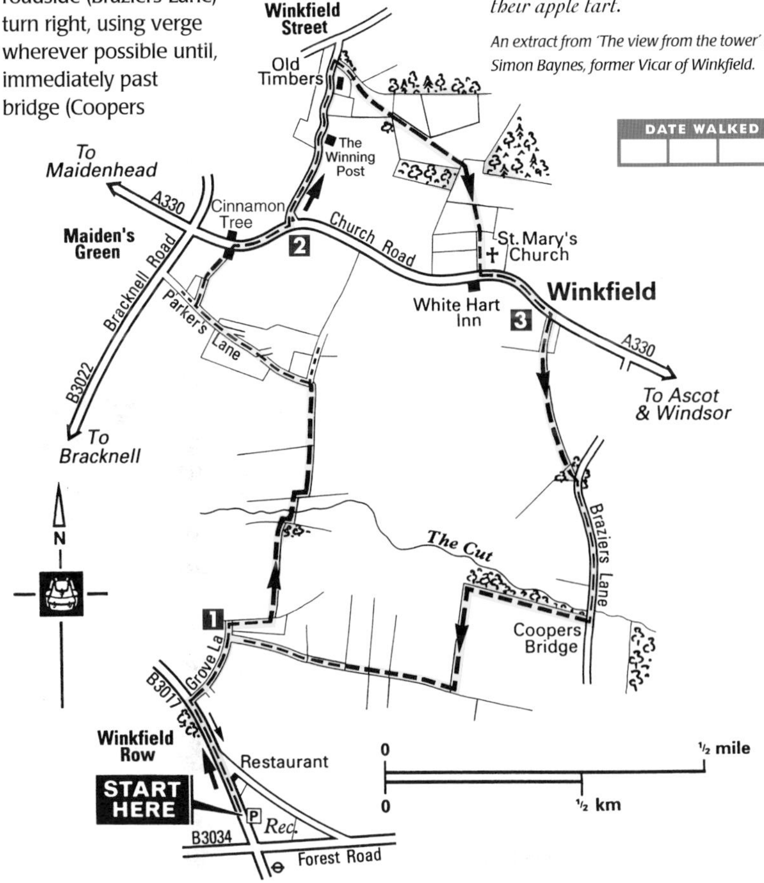

DATE WALKED

Ascot Heath and Great Pond

To many people, Ascot means hats, or horses. But not every day. While this is an opportunity to walk across the world famous racecourse instigated in 1711 by that sporting monarch Queen Anne, it is also a chance to wander through woods and by the huge lake in Sunninghill Park.

Distance: 6 miles / 10 km

OS Map: Explorer 160 Windsor, Weybridge & Bracknell

Start: Car Park No 6 at eastern end of Ascot High St (A329). Not available on racedays. (Grid ref: SU 926 688, Postcode: SL5 7HB)

From car park turn left, then first left along Winkfield Road (A330). After last property on right, Milestone House, turn right into tree-lined path which leads to the Golden Gates. *These gates and adjoining lodge (a listed building) were erected in 1879 at the start of the original straight mile course. This is no longer used for racing, partly because it is invisible from the stands.*

At gates turn left, crossing over road, past Silwood Park Nurseries. At junction with New Mile Ride cross back and continue along left footway until, with Watersplash Lane just ahead, turn into drive past dinky thatched East Lodge (Sunninghill Park). Just before

bottom of curving slope of drive turn left along winding woodland path, over a footbridge, cross a track and go ahead on wide concrete track, beside Great Pond.

1 Continue on this track until finally it passes through Paddock Wood and stops at a field. Go straight across field where a 'rambler stileway' shows the way across Strood Lane (an old road) and on through trees of Wood End. Cross riding track, pass right of cottages and over road just ahead, to turn half-right towards the Loch Fyne restaurant. Before restaurant, turn left down track beside it and left again at road ahead (B3034), then take first turning left, with pointer on tree to Woodside. After blind bend in road followed by several big properties, pass the diminutive 'Rose & Crown', and turn left by the nearby 'Duke of Edinburgh', all part of the hamlet of Woodside.

2 A few yards beyond the 'Duke' turn right into rough track labelled Kiln Lane. *Despite its name, one householder appears to 'fire' concrete balls rather than pots!* At end of houses go straight on, shortly turning right then left, into gated track. Path continues between hedgerow trees/ditch on left and fence on right, leading to swing-gate and stile into field. After another swing-gate in hedge on left follow right-hand side of paddocks (could be very muddy) to emerge at

Late spring morning on the old Coach Road

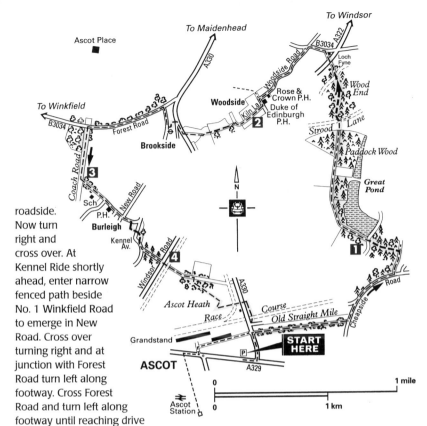

roadside. Now turn right and cross over. At Kennel Ride shortly ahead, enter narrow fenced path beside No. 1 Winkfield Road to emerge in New Road. Cross over turning right and at junction with Forest Road turn left along footway. Cross Forest Road and turn left along footway until reaching drive entrances on both sides of road. Cross over to join footpath at wrought iron pedestrian gate, along drive of Mill Ride Golf Club. *This is an old coach road from an historic property nearby, Ascot Place.*

3 Part way along drive, opposite entrance to stud farm, turn left along hard track, soon becoming roadway and passing school. At second mini-roundabout continue ahead and after side-road on right, go 20 yards on grass verge before forking right into narrow fenced path. Emerging at road cross over, turning right, joining tarmac path beside Kennel Avenue. In front of Old Huntsman's House turn left, along avenue of stately Wellingtonias. *Queen Anne's buckhounds were kennelled near here. You are now following, in reverse direction, a short section of the Three Castles Path, the 60-mile long distance route from Windsor to Winchester, devised by East Berks Ramblers and shown on OS maps.*

At end of Kennel Avenue carefully cross main road and go straight ahead through gate and across racecourse. *If racing is in progress you may be held up for a few minutes but there is free public access to Ascot Heath even on race days.*

4 Follow narrow roadway ahead, looking out for short posts, waymarked 'Three Castles and Church Paths'. Beside cricket pavilion follow these, turning right through parking area to narrow path in left hand corner, then left along attractive section of historic Church Path itself. At minor road follow it right then left, and pass through underpass. Turn right up steps then on level path to reach and cross, via white gates, new straight mile course. Follow tarmac path, descend steps, cross over New Mile Road and keep alongside Winkfield Road to return to start.

DATE WALKED		

Virginia Water and Coworth Park

From the sylvan glades of Windsor Great Park, the impeccable perfection of Coworth Park, to the majestic mansions of Wentworth. Definitely a walk with a wow factor; not really rural, more Ruritania!

Note: Walkers using the public paths across Wentworth Golf Course should be prepared for slight delays when major tournaments are being played.

Distance: 7 miles / 11 km
OS Map: Explorer 160 Windsor, Weybridge & Bracknell
Start: Ascot Station.
(Grid ref: SU 922 683, Postcode: SL5 9EG)
Frequent trains back from Sunninghill Station take 5 minutes. Alternatively, start the walk from Ascot High Street – see Ramble 17 for details.

With your back to main station buildings head left towards footpath signed to Racecourse but at bottom of steps turn sharp left to pass through tunnel under railway. Walk down slope and bear right into All Souls Road,

passing church. Where road swings left, fork off right into woodland footpath. Reaching main road (A330) at road junction cross over, turning right, to end of railing and immediately turn left on path beneath canopy of trees.

1 Emerging at road (Sunninghill) turn right along footway until, shortly beyond railway bridge, turn left into Coombe Lane, passing Tom Green's Field (see companion guide *THREE CASTLES PATH*). At end of this metalled lane carefully cross main road with aid of mirror! Turn right for a few yards, then left into painfully narrow path beside Wellsbridge Cottage.

2 At T-junction turn right, leading up to St Michael's church. *The remarkable hollow yew tree here with its iron girdle is thought to be over 1,000 years old.* Walk through churchyard, with its ornate monuments, to right of church and exit on to lane. Turn left, in front of large burial ground. Go through kissing-gate and along fenced grass strip between fields (known as Church Path). Follow winding path, still fenced, glimpsing lake down through trees on left.

Emerging at road (Buckhurst Road) cross over turning right along footway

Virginia Water

and shortly bear left into Mill Lane and follow this (hopefully) quiet road, fringing Windsor Great Park, to Blacknest Gate. Here turn into park and immediately fork right on surfaced path towards trees, to join tarmac drive at foot of lake. Shortly ahead turn left along lakeside path. Just beyond end of tall trees on left, and just past an Information Board on your left, with view of stone bridge back to left, turn away from lake up gravel path through trees leading to large parking area. Cross to road exit and turn left (A329). Just after large Virginia Water South Car Park sign cross road and face traffic until, at top of slope turn right, signposted Shrubbs Hill, beside Coworth Park signs.

3 Go straight ahead on drive (bridleway) with views across polo grounds to right. *These beautifully kept grounds with a wonderful assortment of architecture both old and new is Coworth Park, reputedly owned by the Sultan of Brunei.* Where the drive reaches (stunning) properties, carefully follow bridleway signs straight ahead, up wooded gulley to left of car park at first and then down to emerge at main road. Here turn left up footway (London Road). At top of hill cross footpath to

Knowle Hill. Follow roadway between palatial properties of Wentworth estate. After crossing one fairway of the course (15th) continue to next open area (large 'SS' on gates nearby). Here turn right onto wide tarmac track. Shortly cross another fairway as right of way continues, now with course nearby through trees on right. Where track forks, bear left and soon at next junction turn right, just before two tall pine trees on either side of the path. Track dips down over another fairway, then levels out through a wood until course appears again on right. When level with a green (12th) turn left over small wooden bridge, then immediately right, on to woodland path.

4 Follow path through light woodland to join road with high hedges concealing houses both sides. Bear left at junction (Heather Drive), turn left (Onslow Road) and shortly cross over (Cobham Road), turning right for only a few paces before turning sharp left into narrow tarmac path. Keep straight ahead along this urban short-cut, until it finally bears left along a roadway (Halfpenny Lane), and leads round a bend to main road. Here turn left along A30 shortly to reach Sunningdale Station.

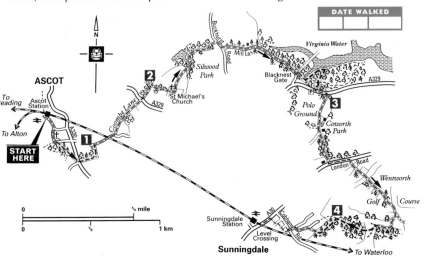

Lily Hill and Swinley Park

Despite the enormous population growth of Bracknell, from 3,000 in 1950 to over 70,000 today, it is still possible to follow a largely 'green' route visiting interesting wildlife sites and a historic hunting forest within a stone's throw of the town.

Distance:	5 miles / 8 km
OS Map:	Explorer 160 Windsor, Weybridge & Bracknell
Start A:	Car park at Longhill Park, Bullbrook, Bracknell. (Grid ref: SU 893 693, Postcode: RG12 9UE)
Start B:	Alternatively, follow the same circuit, starting from Martin's Heron rail station. (Grid ref: SU 888 684, Postcode: RG12 9YY)

Start A: With your back to the road, go straight ahead across park on surfaced path. Where path forks, take right fork and walk round right side of overgrown dell. Soon turn right onto wooden walkway, and at end turn left to leave corner of park down steps. Go ahead, through swing-gate, along cul-de-sac (Timline Green) and turn left up Badgers Way. Cross ahead, over Lily Road and straight up steps to hoggin path into beech woods of Lily Hill Park.

This is one of Bracknell's many Wildlife Heritage Sites. Its 67 acres comprise mixed woodland and parkland. There are some 55 different tree species here which you may like to study more closely another time.

1 At T-junction turn left, then at next T-junction turn left onto tarmac path. Shortly pass some intriguing interpretive wooden 'biscuits' on right, with some benches and a fine viewpoint just below, then very soon turn left uphill at path junction. Near top of slope, fork left between trio of massive 160 year old Wellingtonia trees. Ignore path off to left, but go ahead down to roadside (London Road). Cross at traffic lights and head along the metalled Allsmoor Lane to 'The Cottage' on your right. Round the corner here, turn sharp left after decorated rail-arch and follow tarmac path to Martin's Heron Station.

There are different theories about the origin of this unusual name but in recent times it related to an estate in this area. Its Georgian mansion was demolished in 1983 to make way for new housing.

Passing Matravers' masterpiece!

Start B: From Platform 2 descend railed slope and turn left, to join tarmac path. Admire the superb 'graffiti' – along the right lines for a change!

Go past properties on your right, and turn right on path leading over bridge. At children's play-area turn left (stay on path) and at T-junction turn right onto driveway. Shortly ahead on left pass through metal swing-gate into the shady glades of Swinley Park, part of historic Windsor Forest. *For further details of this area see our THREE CASTLES PATH guide book.*

2 From this gate go ahead along broad ride. Just after first crossing ride, turn left, passing tall pine trees, leading to a 'star' junction. Take the second 'spoke' from left. At next junction of rides take the second exit on right where waymark arrow points the way to exit park beside double wooden gates. Cross road, turning left to walk a short stretch, facing traffic. *Take great care on this narrow, busy road.* Immediately beyond railway bridge, go through wooden gate on right into Englemere Pond Nature Reserve. Shortly ahead, at path crossing (car park to left), turn right. Work continues here to restore the heathland. Follow the red and blue waymarked Nature Trail, soon turning left, to reach Englemere Pond, an ancient feature, ahead. *There is a fine viewing platform here; an ideal place for a rest.*

3 Facing pond turn left on track, soon along a wooden boardwalk, then at T-junction turn right along path known as Butterfly Ride. Shortly ahead, at path junction, our way turns left, then right (keeping timber yard on your right) leading to exit through swing-gate onto London Road (A329).

Cross over at traffic lights, turning left along footway. Try to think beautiful thoughts (winning the Lottery perhaps!) and close your ears to the cacophony of sound along here. Pass the modern buildings of the Licensed Victuallers' School and Hatfield's Garage.

4 Cross Priory Road and at end of brick wall turn right up bank, on a right of way, through a woodland strip. This humble path stays near to fenced green bank, goes round two left-hand bends, finally to emerge at roadside. Turn left and walk up Long Hill Road to the car park.

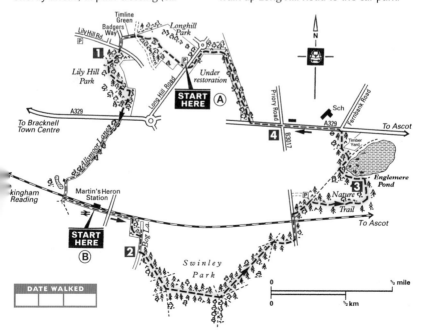

Round Hill and Caesar's Camp

Enjoy this most varied walk, embracing the wide open spaces of Bramshill Forest, the fascinating remains of an Iron Age hill fort and the elegant 18th-century landscape of Easthampstead Park. Can you ask for more?

Distance: 7½ miles / 12 km

OS Map: Explorer 160 Windsor, Weybridge & Bracknell

Start A: Lay-by off Nine Mile Ride, opposite St Sebastian's Memorial Hall, Crowthorne. (Grid ref: SU 832 655, Postcode RG40 3AX)

Start B: Car park at Great Hollands recreation ground, South Road, Bracknell. (Grid ref: SU 851 663, Postcode RG40 3EE)

Start A: With your back to Honey Hill, go half-left into narrow gravel byway with fences on left, soon becoming roadway (Hatch Ride). Follow road to far end (admiring, or otherwise, the changing pattern of domestic

Crowthorne Wood bridleway

architecture over the past 50 years!) At junction, turn right along busy road. Look out for first turning on left, Brookers Row. Here cross over and immediately turn right into an isolated section of Bramshill Forest. Within 50 yards turn left along wide grass ride. Take second track on left, back to gate at roadside, crossing over and turning right along footway.

1 With great care cross road ahead (Bracknell Road) and leaving behind the cacophony of Crowthorne, stride straight ahead along a modest path into another part of Forestry Commission's Bramshill Forest (Crowthorne Woods), soon beside tall pines. Shortly turn left onto broad rising forest track. At prominent meeting of ways (top of Round Hill) take the bridleway bearing half-right, rising more steeply, up to a staggered crossing; go a few feet left to continue on the same line. Now on minor path through trees, shortly drop down steeply to the historic track known as the Devil's Highway. *This is the route of a Roman road from Silchester to London.*

Turn left along the 'Highway'. Shortly ahead, modern man has made his mark by bridging the Roman way. Just after passing under bridge, disregard wire-fenced footpath, but turn next left to climb winding path up tree-covered slope. On the top it straightens out, with younger trees on right. At first crossing path, bear right along prominent track. At next crossing, take path straight ahead (between trees) which curves left. Meeting a very prominent crossing, turn right. Then at next junction of rides, go on through avenue of trees and go ahead and cross stile into southern entrance of Caesar's Camp.

2 Follow wide track ahead through middle of camp, at one point passing just left of tree-cloaked steep bank and ditch. Our way descends Queen Anne Gully (cut through the ramparts in 1702), swinging left at bottom to cross stile by metal gate. Continue downhill until a few yards before another gate, turn left onto path in trees with road close by on right. Follow this path for a distance, finally crossing road to join start of metalled footway on the other side. At roundabout cross Crowthorne Road and continue on footway. Just beyond bus stop turn right into woodland strip. Keep left of houses ahead and shortly bear left along broad avenue of trees with rhododendrons at their feet. Cross over (South Road) and turn right on path beside road.

Start B: From car park cross road to footway, turning right.

3 Pass cemetery and continue on verge beside tall conifers. At T-junction bear right, to follow golf course boundary fence, through a metal gate and on until the path turns left and becomes a wide tarmac pathway.

Continue straight on to pass school and enter drive, gated at far end. Now take right fork in road ahead and shortly, where this bears right, go straight ahead on footpath. Path now follows field-edge beside tree-lined ditch.

4 At T-junction turn left, go straight across splendid tree-lined main drive of Easthampstead Park. Ahead pass farmhouse to join wide tarmac drive (part of Ramblers Route) leading to road. Here carefully cross over, turn right for 30 yards, then left over stile to another on far side of field. Turn right along road (Easthampstead Road) for about 250 yards before turning left at swing-gate. Head diagonally across two fields (with stile between) to footbridge in far corner. Go straight across next field to another bridge. Waymarked track ahead loops round past Honey Hill Housing Development and at road turn left along Honey Hill back to start.

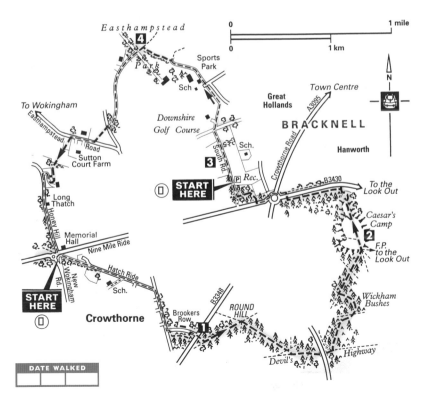

DATE WALKED

Chapel Green and Luckley Path

How wonderful it is to be able to walk from the centre of Wokingham to open countryside within a few minutes. The railways east and south of the town have acted as a buffer in holding back the tide of development. This gentle stroll explores a green corridor with barely a sign of habitation. Wander while you may!

Distance: 4½ miles / 7 km
OS Map: Explorer 159 Reading, Wokingham and Pangbourne
Start: Wokingham Library, off Denmark Street.
(Grid ref: SU 811 683, Postcode: RG40 2BB) See map for link with station.

Admire 'Waterbabies' sculpture at main entrance to library, then turn left down slope and left again on footway of Denmark Street. At mini-roundabout cross over, pass Dukes Head, then straight on down Finchampstead Road towards, and under, railway bridge. Just before next roundabout turn into footpath by two houses on left. After gate follow gravelled track. At parking area go half-right up between paddocks to pass Chapel Green Farm followed shortly by Lucas Hospital.

This splendid building of 1665 is owned by the Drapers' Company and is the only Grade 1 listed building in Wokingham.
1 Admire the house from the main gate then continue on footpath straight ahead, go round clump of holly and head across small meadow to leave through gap near right-hand corner. Turn right along tarmac drive leading away from Ludgrove School, *a preparatory school whose 'old boys' include Princes William and Harry.* A few strides beyond white pillars turn left beside metal gates into footpath, posing here as a wide gravel track which reveals occasional glimpses of the hospital back across the fields. After some distance the track swings left, away from the Wokingham/Guildford railway, shortly to pass gate before property on right.
2 After cottage take first on right, by gate, becoming a wide track, soon through an open area. *It is easy to visualise the once tree-less heath that existed here before the land was enclosed in 1817. Today it is managed by the Forestry Commission.* Eventually track bears left and, shortly, left again at junction.

'The Waterbabies' – our start point outside Wokingham Library

Some 75 yards after this second bend, bear left into path through trees. Keep straight on, ignoring path off to left, until emerging from trees. Continue ahead now on broad gravel track (a line we shall follow for more than a mile back to Wokingham). Keep straight on over two prominent crossing tracks, followed by wooden footbridge, to an open ditch marking end of woodland.

3 Now continue ahead between Grays Farm fruit growing fields at first. Path then narrows between fences, becoming grassy. Look out for sports field on left and at its end, with gate just ahead, fork left into narrow path with field on left. At gateway cross drive (to Ludgrove School). *The route we are following is known as Luckley Path and has existed for over 500 years. Notice shortly ahead small bridge over the diminutive Emm Brook, a reminder of the many tanneries which stood on its banks when leather was a major industry in the town.*

The path ahead rises and crosses footbridge over railway (Reading/Waterloo line). Turn left along road (Gipsy Lane) for some 50 yards, then turn right on path beside row of lime trees, *marking the only remaining part of one-time Langborough common field.*

4 Cross ahead at start of Howard Road, then keep straight on along fenced path before turning left through the attractive Howard Palmer Gardens (recalling a member of the Reading biscuit-making family).

Leaving Park, cross car park. To return to library, turn left down narrow walled path (Cockpit Path) and across lower parking area. If returning to station, do not turn left but go straight ahead, leading to Market Place and Town Hall (see map).

DATE WALKED

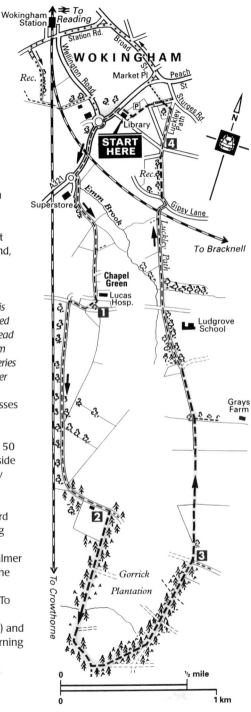

Maidenhead to Windsor

Step this way for a great escape (from a town), a brief encounter (with an unspoilt village), reach a historic climax (the largest inhabited castle in the world) – then return by train!

Distance: 7¼ miles / 12 km
OS Map: Explorer 172 Chiltern Hills East, Explorer 160 Windsor, Weybridge & Bracknell
Start: Maidenhead Station (Grid ref: SU 887 807, Postcode: SL6 1EW)
Finish: Windsor Central Station

From station main entrance walk down left side of forecourt, turn right, pass under railway bridge and cross over roadways ahead. Turn left into paved footway, signed Retail Park, which turns right in front of multi-storey car park. At road ahead (Stafferton Way) turn left and cross over at pedestrian lights. Turn right beside Lidl on tarmac path signed 'Green Way' and 'Braywick Park'.

At T-junction by bridge, turn right on roadway, soon becoming track. After squeeze-way go straight on with high bank on left. After some 250 yards, where minor paths branch off both sides, just past bench on left, turn left up slope and bear right to follow faint grass path along

crest of high ground. Path leads down through gap in fences to steps. At foot of steps, turn right to cross footbridge and at meeting of paths take first on left, in front of bench, to squeeze-way at road. Carefully cross over turning right, then shortly left (still 'Green Way') by group of pretty Victorian cottages. Pass between white rails into tree-lined Causeway which crosses stream (The Cut) and leads to Bray village.

1 Turn right for a few yards along High Street, then cross into entrance drive of 14th century St Michael's Church, whose turncoat vicar is recalled in the well known lines:

> *And this is law, I will maintain*
> *Until my dying day, Sir;*
> *That whatsoever King may reign,*
> *I'll still be the Vicar of Bray, Sir.*

Pass to right of church and leave graveyard in far right corner. Emerging at road (Ferry Road) turn left to view famous Thames-side restaurant, The Waterside Inn. Retrace steps from slipway and turn left in front of black and white terrace, Bettoney Vere, leading to Old Mill Lane then use the tree-lined, roadside path – becoming Monkey Island Lane. Cross motorway bridge and continue along road until, just before the bridge over The Cut, turn left onto permitted path. Follow this to cross the Thames by footbridge.

There was until recently a conveyor bridge here, built to carry the 4 million tonnes of soil and gravel extracted to create

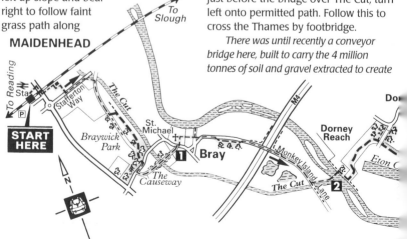

MAIDENHEAD

To Slough

To Reading

To Sta...

P

START HERE

Braywick Park

The Cut

St. Michael

1 **Bray**

The Causeway

N

M4

Dorney Reach

Do...

Monkey Island Lane

The Cut

2

Eton C...

Eton College's 2 km long eight-lane rowing lake that hosted the rowing events at the London 2012 Olympics. The development also includes a 400 acre area of parkland that walkers may wish to explore later.

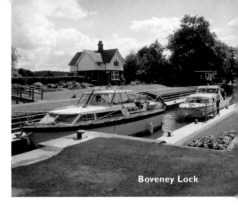
Boveney Lock

2 On far side of river turn downstream for about 100 yards then left to follow waymarked path. Presently bear right (signed Windsor and Eton) through gate to cross access road. Continue on long winding path with bridleway on left. Some kissing-gates that we pass give access to an area overlooking the rowing lake.

3 Some distance after passing lakes and Archaeological Information Board on right, just before the path gives an open view of the rowing trench, our way turns sharp left over a stile next to a gate onto Dorney Common. Head across Common, aiming for stand of tall trees, directly ahead on other side of road. Cross road some 25 yards to left of 'Bend' road sign and follow faint path by hedgerow and ditch to reach stile on right hand side of these trees. Follow broad strip between fields (Roasthill Lane), turn right at path T-junction, then left down chestnut tree lined drive to reach river by Boveney Lock.

Staying on the river-side footpath, walk downstream until immediately after footbridge (Boveney Ditch); here turn left for a few paces, then take the farthest right mid-field way, first over meadow and then crop field, aiming for the archways (A355) in the distance. When joining permanent bridleway keep right and stay on this track

towards the archways, with pinnacles of Eton College chapel beyond. After tunnel, go straight ahead, and under the rail viaduct. *The line opened in 1849, the viaduct being built of brick in 1865. To discourage ideas of truancy, Eton College erected a 10ft high wall!*

4 On far side of arch go slightly right over grass towards cluster of tall chestnut trees and walk through line of trees. Tarmac path ahead crosses two playing fields, with road between them; then goes straight on through car park, to reach road leading into High Street, Eton. Here turn right over river-bridge and go straight ahead at traffic lights up Thames Street, opposite castle walls, to find, almost at top of hill, Central Station on right in the shopping precinct. To return to Maidenhead by rail, catch a train from here and change at Slough. Alternatively, catch a bus at the top of Thames Street.

DATE WALKED		

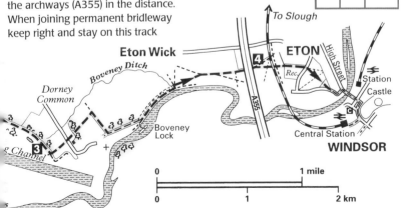

Wick Hill and Longwater Lane

A wonderful variety of woodland and river valley scenery all within the parish of Finchampstead. Explore the National Trust protected slopes of The Ridges and visit the Saxon hilltop church of St James.

Distance:	6½ miles / 10 km
OS Map:	Explorer 159 Reading, Wokingham & Pangbourne
Start:	Car park behind shops by double mini-roundabouts at junction of Finchampstead Road (B3016) and Nine Mile Ride, south of Wokingham. (Grid ref: SU 797 647, Postcode: RG40 3RB)

Leaving car park turn right, then right again along Nine Mile ride. Shortly fork right into gravelled Wick Hill Lane, which steadily rises. At top of rise take left fork. Path ahead narrows, then turns right onto surfaced path past large modern houses. Surfaced drive becomes rough track and continues through light woodland until emerging by cluster of properties, passing Tudor Cottage.

1 Follow drive (passing walled cottage garden) until at road junction (B3348) cross into Dell Road and descend, with some pleasant views on

Enjoy the view from this rising field-edge path

a clear day. Look out on left for an unusually large holly tree. Almost at bottom of slope take footpath on left between Ridgewood and Warren Cottage. At end of garden look out for small stone engraved '1913' marking start of Finchampstead Ridges. *The Ridges is one of the Trust's earliest acquisitions, the first 60 acres having been purchased by public subscription for £3,000, part of the Bearwood Estate owned by the Walter family, one-time owners of 'The Times' newspaper.*

2 To ensure correct route, from the engraved stone count 175 (!) good strides, straight up path to a junction. (Two steeply ascending paths visible ahead.) Here take the path turning right at 90 degrees (immediately in front of a large silver birch), to follow a well-used route, beside narrow ditch on left at first, staying roughly on the same contour of the hill. Continue on, following main path, ignoring paths joining from left and right. Path crosses two short walkways, runs alongside wooden fence and then turns right beside wire fence, leading to exit from NT woodland. Turn right down track, passing The Old Thatch, to reach and turn right along a quiet lane, Lower Sandhurst Road.

3 Reaching car park, turn left to join footpath beside lake leading to Blackwater River, county boundary with Hampshire. Turn right, over small footbridge, and along riverbank for a distance. Fork right in front of small sewage works, where path swings away to road (Longwater Road) at swing-gate. Cross over into field opposite, turning left along narrow ribbon of a gravel path as it winds round two sides of gravel pit close to ditch, to arrive at swing-gate and footbridge. Here turn right up hedged path between fields (Longwater Lane). Just past start of houses, to continue walk turn left, but first go ahead for about 20 paces to wooden signpost on left where a plaque gives details of an incident involving King Henry VII back in 1501. Retracing your steps, follow climbing path with fence on right, to emerge at road called The Village (B3348).

4 Turn right past garage and cross over road, shortly to enter playing-field gates near phone box. Take a line half-right, to pass play-area, towards top left corner of field and join adjacent hedged track. Turn left and follow this to reach, after swing-gate and several steps, the Saxon parish church of St James on its man-made mound. Pass left of church and down path to gate.

Notice immediately on left plaque in wall to George V and nearby red oak. Ahead on the green once stood an oak marking Queen Victoria's first 50 years on the throne (see stone in ivy mound) and across road on right is another, marking her death in 1901. At that time the pub here changed its name from White Horse to

Queen's Oak, and now claims to be the only one of that name in the country.

5 Pass in front of the pub and on along road (Church Lane). Just beyond Church Farm Bungalow turn left at stile on diagonal line across field to stile at road. Cross carefully, turning left, then immediately right, through a wooden swing-gate. Enjoy this open, rising, field-edge path with its fine view looking back towards the church and after further swing-gate soon reach junction which completes our circuit. Here turn left down Wick Hill and retrace your steps back to the start.

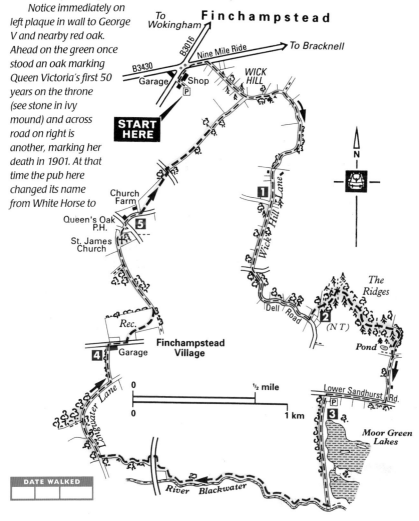

Finchampstead

To Wokingham

To Bracknell

B3016

Nine Mile Ride

B3430

WICK HILL

Garage Shop

P

START HERE

Church Farm

Queen's Oak P.H.

5

St. James Church

Wick Hill Lane

1

N

The Ridges

Dell Road

2

(N T)

Pond

Rec.

4 Garage

Finchampstead Village

Lower Sandhurst Rd.

P

3

Longwater Lane

0 ——— ½ mile

0 ——— 1 km

Moor Green Lakes

DATE WALKED

River Blackwater

Ambarrow Hill and Finchampstead Ridges

A chance to sample some of the surviving areas of traditional heathland, managed today by the National Trust, around the beautiful and popular Finchampstead Ridges. Explore the slopes of Ambarrow Hill or perhaps picnic in the adjoining Country Park.

Distance: 4 miles / 6 km

OS Map: Explorer 159 Reading, Wokingham and Pangbourne

Start: Crowthorne Station. (Grid ref: SU 823 638, Postcode: RG45 6DF) See map for alternative start at Ambarrow Court, avoiding high parking charges at Station (Grid ref: SU 825 626, Postcode: GU47 8JD)

With your back to the main station buildings, turn right into St Francis Close and follow footway through gate passing to left of flats ahead. After offices, path continues ahead with woodland on left. Reaching embankment of bridge (over railway) ahead, bear left and shortly turn right, to follow fenced path beside sports field (part of Bracknell's Ramblers' Route). Just after entering woodland ahead, turn right through metal swing-gate to cross railway, into NT 11 acre pine-clad woodland of Ambarrow Hill. *Is this cone-shaped hill a natural feature or could it be man-made? Nobody seems to know!*

1 Fifty yards ahead there are three choices: 1. To turn left into the grounds of one-time Victorian mansion, Ambarrow Court, now a country park. 2. Bear right to climb and explore Ambarrow Hill. 3. To continue walk, by staying on path ahead between holly bushes at first, along foot of hill until, just before road ahead turn left, leading to car park. Here carefully cross road (A321) and join footpath along edge of woodland strip. Continue ahead along lane until, just past drive on right to

Heath Pond